YOUR KNOWLEDGE HA

- We will publish your bachelor's and
  master's thesis, essays and papers

- Your own eBook and book -
  sold worldwide in all relevant shops

- Earn money with each sale

Upload your text at www.GRIN.com
and publish for free

The Effect of the "Internet of Things" on Supply Chain Integration and Performance. An Organizational Capability Perspective in the Automotive Industry

Albert Adusei Brobbey

Bibliographic information published by the German National Library:

The German National Library lists this publication in the National Bibliography; detailed bibliographic data are available on the Internet at http://dnb.dnb.de.

ISBN: 9783346737083
This book is also available as an ebook.

© GRIN Publishing GmbH
Nymphenburger Straße 86
80636 München

Print and binding: Books on Demand GmbH, Norderstedt, Germany
Printed on acid-free paper from responsible sources.

The present work has been carefully prepared. Nevertheless, authors and publishers do not incur liability for the correctness of information, notes, links and advice as well as any printing errors.

GRIN web shop: https://www.grin.com/document/1281134

THE EFFECT OF "INTERNET OF THINGS" ON SUPPLY CHAIN INTEGRATION AND PERFORMANCE: AN ORGANISATIONAL CAPABILITY PERSPECTIVE IN THE AUTOMOTIVE INDUSTRY.

By

Albert Adusei Brobbey

ABSTRACT

The Internet of things (IoT) is a next generation of Internet connected embedded ICT systems in a digital environment to seamlessly integrate supply chain and logistics processes. Integrating emerging IoT into the current ICT systems can be unique because of its intelligence, autonomous and pervasive applications for better organizational performance. This study explored the effect of IoT on supply chain integration and performance in the automotive industry of Germany. The dataset comprises a quantitative survey and a sample size of 50 employees in the automotive industry of Germany. The obtained data from a structured questionnaire, which was built on a 5-point Likert scale, was analyzed by the use of Linear Regression. The analysis of the study was enacted by using STATA (15.0) statistical software to excerpt the results. The proposed model was blueprinted based on relationship marketing theory, resource-based view theory, contingency theory, and related literature. Before estimating the main results, preliminary analysis such as descriptive statistics, correlation analysis, validity and reliability of the instruments, multi-collinearity test and model fitness were done to provide initial justification and appropriateness of the instruments and the methods chosen to test the proposed relationships guiding the study. The outcome of the study revealed that Internet of Thing had a significant and positive effect on supply chain integration in the Mercedes automotive industry, Germany. Again, the findings of this study indicate that Internet of Thing had a significant positive effect on performance in the Mercedes automotive industry, Germany. Consequentially, this study has found out that supply chain integration has significant and positive effect on performance in the Mercedes automotive industry of Germany.

Keywords: Internet of Things, supply chain integration, performance, organizational capability theory and system theory

CONTENTS

LIST OF TABLES

CHAPTER ONE

INTRODUCTION

1.1 Background of the Study

In recent years, Internet of Things and supply chain integration have witnessed tremendous paradigm shifts (De Vass, et al 2018). The increasing interest in Internet of Things and supply chain integration has been driven by competitive pressure and has led to its eventual elevation to critical part of organizational operations and strategy (Rejeb, et al 2020). The roles of Internet of Things and supply chain integration as organizational functions have become more pronounced in sustaining their competitive position in this increasingly dynamic business environment (Tang, & Veelenturf, 2019). Organizations have to continuously upgrade their Internet of Things and supply chain integration in order to deliver the right product to the right customer at the right time (Rejeb, et al 2020).

Internet of Things (IoT) is defined as a universal platform of Internet-connected smart objects that allow things to connect anytime, anywhere using any network or service (De Vass, et al 2018). It is advancement in technological innovation connecting objects and devices through Internet (De Vass, et al 2018). The network of objects embedded with sensors and software has the potential to collect and communicate data over internet (Rejeb, et al 2020). Internet of Things and supply chain integration platform facilitate things to be identified, located, sensed and controlled via the global platform. It is viewed as progression of information and communication technology (ICT) applications that are helpful to capture and share data in a network of organizations on real-time basis (De Vass, et al 2018). This digitally upgrading of conventional objects via internet connectivity generates added capabilities to its functionality. Internet of Things may differ to

1

previous ICT capabilities due to their ubiquity, intelligence and autonomy (Mohanty and Mishra 2020).

The Internet of Things is the next generation of internet-connected embedded ICT systems to integrate supply chain process in a digital environment. Because of its intelligence and pervasive applications, the integration of emerging of Internet of Things into the current ICT systems can be unique (Cruz, 2021). It is viewed as an extension of legacy ICT systems that facilitate information sharing among individuals, organizations, and industries (Borgia, 2014). Internet of Things (IoT) has become an imported part of company performance in any company around the world, irrespective of its ideology, culture, religion. Additionally, it can be said supply chain integration with IoT has a critical factor to influence the company performance. Thus, the platform facilitates the identification, location, sensing and control of "things" through the global platform (Borgia, 2014). It is viewed as advancing information and communication technology (ICT) applications that are useful in capturing and sharing data in real-time networks of organizations (De Vass, et al 2018).The technical reason for promoting the supply chain insole the need to improve the quality of the life as reflected by IoT, increasing opportunities for enhancing the company performance and the need to absorbed the consuming time on the production and commutation with the customer, employee, Supplier.

1.2 Problem Statement

Supply chain is primarily demand driven, intense digital connectivity and coordination via adoption of new technology can be considered as an intervention in improving performance. The emerging IoT paradigm plays a significant role in organizations to manage supply networks in response to customer demands (De Vass, et al 2018). Moreover, the supply chain literature on IoT

2

application is broadly rhetoric, technology and architecture focused and quite nascent (Mishra et al., 2016). Due to enthusiasm on technological adoption in data transparency and visibility to achieve supply chain process integration, the research on IoT within this context is timely (Tu, 2018). Aside conventional ICT technologies help monitor supply chain functions such as purchasing, transportation, storage, distribution, sales and returns, many other smart devices recently joining the list under the newly coined Internet of Things umbrella of technologies, the potential to address the information capture and exchange in real-time has multiplied (De Vass, et al 2018; Vanpoucke, et al., 2017).

Although the advances in Internet of Things applications is expected to revolutionize retail sectors, its acceptance and potential to integrate supply chain processes is largely under developed both for theoretical and practical implications (Kahlert et al 2017). Again, there have been a number of studies that have investigated the ICT-enabled supply chain processes integration in improving the performance, however, little studies are documented to empirically assess the effect of emerging Internet of Things on supply chain integration (Vanpoucke et al., 2017). Also, Internet of Things has increased as a creative innovation with volumes to progress inventory network data stream, stand that as it might, the influence of Internet of Things on supply chain integration and thus execution is not yet been thoroughly investigated (De Vass, et al 2018). Theoretically, in the global literature sense, a number of studies have been done in more developed economies on the various facets of Internet of Things and supply chain integration such as Europe, America, Asia and the Western world (Mohanty & Mishra 2020). However, the impact of Internet of Things on supply chain integration and performance in the automotive industry is limited and is still unclear.

3

1.3 Research Objectives

This study seeks to examine the effect of internet of things on supply chain integration and performance. In assuring that the above objective can be achieved, few specific objectives need to be accomplished. These specific objectives are as follows:

(i)   To examine the relationships between internet of things and supply chain integration in the Mercedes automotive industry.

(ii)   To examine the relationships between internet of things and performance in the Mercedes automotive industry.

(iii)   To examine the relationships between supply chain integration and performance in the Mercedes automotive industry.

1.4 Research Questions

For the above objectives to be achieved, the study will attempt to answer the following questions.

(i)   Does internet of things has a significant effect on supply chain integration in the Mercedes automotive industry?

(ii)   Does internet of things has a significant effect on performance in the Mercedes automotive industry?

(iii)   Does supply chain integration has a significant effect on performance in the Mercedes automotive industry?

1.5 Significance of the Study

This study certainly serves as a springboard for other studies into the field of internet of things, supply chain integration and performance especially in the automotive industry that has seen intense competition. The outcome of this research also holds significant benefits for researchers and practitioners who are interested in internet of things with the useful knowledge and in-depth overview of IoT and supply chain integration. Theoretically, this study empirically validates the positive effect of IoT on supply chain integration to improve performance by testing a conceptual framework. This study also provides detailed evidence of how IoT technologies influence supply chain integration and firm performance. Also, this research enlightens practitioners, policy makers and industry associations that IoT technologies enable information capture that can be helpful in decision making. The study finishes practitioners that investment in IoT technologies is a strategic move for better integration of supply chain partners for inventory status and market demand.

1.6 Brief Methodology

This research was conducted by employing the following methodologies in collecting and analyzing the data. Data was collected from the employees of automotive industry in Mercedes, Germany. Considering the research objectives and hypotheses, quantitative research method is employed and considered appropriate since it facilitates the examination of the hypotheses. This study also employs the deductive reasoning approach, which develops hypotheses from existing expertise and tests them through empirical observations (Andreev *et al,.* 2009). The hypotheses were tested based on empirical data using SPSS and STATA software. Consequentially, preliminary analytical procedures were undertaken to check the following: (a) the appropriateness of the data distribution (b) exploratory factor analysis (EFA) to examine the appropriateness, factor

5

extraction (c) test for internal consistency and reliability, (d) tests of multi-collinearity among explanatory variables. Lastly, the hypotheses were tested for direct relationships using multiple linear regression models.

1.7 Structure of the Study

The thesis is consisted of five (5) chapters which was organized as follows: Chapter one provided a general overview of the entire study that is; background of the study, problem statement, aim and objectives, research questions and the significance of the study. Chapter two presented the literature review. The chapter reviewed literature on internet of thing, supply chain integration and performance. Chapter three provides discussion of the methodology adopted for the research. It also outlined the research design for the study. Chapter four also provides an in-depth analysis, presentation, and interpretation of results of all the data collected for the study in relation to the research objectives and questions mentioned in chapter one. The final chapter, Chapter five comprised of the conclusion, recommendations, limitations and other avenues for further research.

CHAPTER TWO

LITERATURE REVIEW

2.0 Introduction

This chapter encompasses of the literature relating to the topic. This will comprise of both the theoretical, conceptual and empirical literature of evaluating the effect of Internet of Thing on supply chain integration and performance. It further discusses the theories underlying the study of Internet of Thing, supply chain integration and performance as well as the conceptual framework.

2.1 The Internet of Things (IoT)

Internet of Thing pertains to an extension or a new version of generic ICT (Borgia 2014), an evolution from internetworked computers to internetworked objects connecting previously unconnected "things" (De Vass, 2018). Uckelmann, et al., (2011) conceptualise IoT as a virtual world of ICT integrated seamlessly with the real world things. The IoT core concept was pioneered in 1999, when the Auto-ID Center of MIT used radio frequency identification tags with a unique electronic product code as a tool to identify and track supply chain commodities via the Internet platform (Verdouw et al. 2016). Although IoT originates from radio frequency identification, it is now a central element on its own with far reaching capabilities (Borgia 2014). The notion of IoT has evolved by complementing further competences such as sensory, context awareness, intelligence, pervasiveness, learning ability and automation to reach its conceptualized unlimited potentials (Kahlert et al. 2017). IoT is not a singular novel technology, but rather a collection of several complementary technologies that provide extended capabilities (Lee & Lee 2015). IoT has

7

the potential to dramatically change our lives by making many impossible things possible, by connecting everything on the earth together via the Internet. Therefore, IoT is seen as a disruptive technology, due to the fundamental changes it is reported to generate. IoT uses the Internet as a global platform for devices to communicate, coordinate, compute and dialogue with each other (Miorandi et al. 2012). The capabilities and intelligence of IoT devices is posited to exceed the in-built functionalities of the device itself by using the Internet as a communication infrastructure, storage mechanism and a medium for data processing and information synthesis (De Vass, 2018).

2.2 Supply Chain Integration (SCI)

Supplier integration is defined as the coordination and information sharing with suppliers that provide the focal firm with insights into suppliers' processes, capabilities and constraints, ultimately enabling more effective planning and forecasting, product and process design, and transaction management (De Vass, 2018). It is the extent to which a firm collaborates with suppliers to configure inter-firm practices, behaviours, procedures and strategies into synchronised, practicable and cooperative processes to meet customer demand (Huo 2012). Integration implemented in the supply chain, with the aim of collaborating with other supply chain partners, is to have a free flow of information and resources to manage both the intra and inter-organization processes and to ensure a smooth flow of operations. The aim of supply chain integration is to have a free flow of information or resources or money or products and services to serve customers in an efficient and effective manner. This, in turn, influences rapid organizational processes and reduces operating costs (De Vass, 2018). It also encourages supply chain patterns for strategic collaboration and provides both operational and strategic benefits. It encourages supply chain partners to share information, reduce risks in the supply chain and accelerate the

8

duration of the contract and enhance trust between the partners (Huo 2012). It highlights the importance and outcomes of both the inter-organizational and intra-organizational processes. The objective is to achieve both operational and organizational performance. Supplier and customer integration refers to strategic common management, information sharing and in general collaboration between suppliers and customers (Yu et al., 2017). In order to obtain successful supply chain integration a system that joins all the information retrieved along every step of the supply chain is necessary. Supply chain integration is the last step of a successful IoT implementation. It is a cloud-based platform for business collaboration, which is based on a common set of Internet technology (Verdouw, et al., 2014).

2.3 Performance

According to Agwu, (2018) performance is the total wellbeing of an organization matching its results against assets committed to achieving the set goals. It is the attainment of organizational strategic goals (Almatroshi et al., 2016). It is the process of assessing the profitability, market share, increase of return on investment, increase of customer satisfaction, an increase of customer retention, and sales growth of an organization (Battor & Battor, 2010). It is the output-input ratio in the organization, the degree of target achievement, and the satisfaction of participants in the organizational process. One major issue that hems most managers is how their organizations perform in the marketplace (Tseng et al., 2013). Therefore, managers consider it as a fantastic management strategy (Gupta & Wales, 2017). Generally, the multifaceted nature of performance has gained the heed of researchers with multiple opinions on the most right way to measure performance (Gupta & Wales, 2017). The main objective of evaluating the performance is to define the difference between real and desired results and to determine the efficiency and effectiveness

9

of the process. Performance measurement guided the organization to achieve a double improvement and an accurate evaluation of the benefits achieved. Performance indicators take into account sales and efficiency. It allows the shareholder to know the long-term success of the business and how it serves its own clients on the market. Understanding the aspects will make a company effective in providing good product quality to meet consumer expectations (Wisner et al., 2010).

2.4 The relationship between Internet of Thing and supply chain integration

The literature reports that IoT, as an extension of ICT (Borgia 2014), also has the extended ability to assist with real-time information flow thereby facilitating inter- and intra-firm communication to further integrate supply chains. The way Internet connects computers, IoT platform has the capability to potentially connect products, machines and people in sync, therefore coordinating and integrating the internal and external activities of an enterprise (Li & Li 2017).

Studies have long-established the positive relationships between ICT and supplier integration. Moreover, as per organizational capability theory, ICT as a core capability can positively influence supplier integration (Huo 2012). Studies have also found that while ICT does not have a direct relationship with performance ICT affects performance through its positive effect on SCI (Kim 2017). Vanpoucke et al. 2017; Zhang et al. 2011) from multidimensional angle, find IoT to be a crucial enabler for all three dimensions of SCI, namely supplier, internal and customer integration. Therefore they conclude that IoT, as a progression of ICT can enhance supplier, internal and customer integration capability. De Vass et al., (2018) studied the effect of Internet of Things on supply chain integration and performance. They draw upon the organizational capability theory for developing an empirical model considering the effect of IoT capabilities on multiple

10

dimensions of supply chain process integration, and in turn improve supply chain performance as well as organizational performance. Cross-sectional survey data from 227 Australian retail firms was analyzed using structural equation modeling (SEM). The results indicate that IoT capability has a positive and significant effect on internal, customer-, and supplier-related process integration that in turn positively affects supply chain performance and organizational performance. Naser, H. A. N. (2019) examines the adoption of IoT in the supply chain environment and its reflection on the supply and company performance. Finding analysis reveals IoT added capacity which increases the transparency of the supply chain, auto-capture and sharing of information for greater SCI. The integration technology IoT demonstrates a positive impact on the entire supply chain's price, efficiency, distribution, and versatility and increases the sustainable performance of retail companies with performance, social, and environmental outcomes. Based on the above literature, we therefore hypothesize that:

H1: *Internet of Thing has a positive effect on supply chain integration.*

2.5 The relationship between Internet of Thing and performance

IoT is an emerging global Internet-based information service architecture facilitating the exchange of goods in global supply chain networks by generating value for all partners in order to improve performance (Lee & Lee, 2015). As an extended ICT capability, IoT is increasingly adopted to further improve performance (Borgia 2014). IoT can optimise how people and systems interact to coordinate their activities to better performance. Analytics can be applied to make improvements and promote best practices for greater performance across the entire IoT operational efficiency, safety and security and customer experience (Ben Daya et al. 2017). ICT capability is also likely to influence performance through quality improvements, enhanced productivity and utilization,

11

reduced waste and ultimately, increased supply chain efficiency and effectiveness. Academic literature has provided enough empirical evidence on the relationship between IoT and performance, or the effect of IoT capability on SCI the mediation link theorized to be paramount for performance. However, there is emerging consensus about this omission (Ben-Daya et al. 2017; Mishra et al. 2016). Therefore, empirical examinations on whether IoT can strengthen SCI to influence performance have been thoroughly studied (De Vass, et al., 2018; Verdouw et al. 2016). Based on the above empirical studies, we hypothesize that:

H2: Internet of Thing has a positive effect on performance

2.6 The relationship between supply chain integration and performance

From the organizational capability theory perspective, a firm's integration capability is viewed as a dynamic organizational capability that has a direct effect on performance (Huo 2012). The theory suggests that integration prevents opportunistic behaviours, curtails production and transaction costs and enhances resource obtainability, while facilitating knowledge sharing among supply chain partners, consequently improving the ability to cope with environmental uncertainty (Huo 2012). Literature suggests that partner integration can minimize costs via waste reduction and asset utilization and also help supply chains to be more flexible, adaptive, reactive and responsive to cope with risks and market uncertainty hence improves performance (Reaidy et al. 2015). Literature further suggests that supply chain integration impacts organizational performance positively (Vanpoucke et al., 2017). The real time information provided by IoT helps track supply chain activities, from product design to the end users, providing accurate and timely information to help organizations respond to the market changes (Mishra et al., 2016). While supply chain strategy yields performance by focusing on cost, quality, delivery and flexibility improvement, it

12

attempts to align with the firm objectives of improving performance to generate environmental, social, and economic benefits (Owuso, & Jaja, 2022). De Vass et al., (2018) studied the effect of Internet of Things on supply chain integration and performance. Cross-sectional survey data from 227 Australian retail firms was analyzed using structural equation modeling (SEM). The results indicate that supply chain integration has a positive and significant effect on organizational performance. De Vass, (2018). Examines the effect if Internet of Things enabled on supply chain integration and performance using mixed method investigation of the Australian retail industry. The results reveal that IoT capability is perceived to have a positive influence on internal and external process integration that, in turn, positively affects supply chain and firm performance. Further, IoT-enabled external integration was perceived to influence supply chain performance significantly more than IoT-enabled internal integration. The following studies also found a positive relationship between supply chain integration and performance (Owuso, & Jaja, 2022; Vanpoucke et al. 2017; Prajogo & Olhager 2012). From the empirical studies above, we hypothesize that:

H3: Supply chain integration has a positive effect on performance

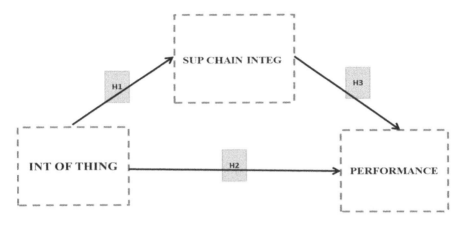

Figure 2.1: Conceptual framework of the study

2.7 Related Theories

This point presents the theoretical foundations that guide the study of the effect of IoT on supply

chain integration and performance in the automotive industry. The two main theories underpinning

this work are organizational capability theory and system theory.

2.7.1 Organizational Capability Theory

IoT adoption can be viewed as an additional capability that may add value to the current

configuration of ICT capability within any organization. It is important for studies to utilize and

treat IoT as a progression of ICT capability that may facilitate intra- and inter organizational

communication and information flows in more integrated way (Borgia, 2014). The intra- and inter

organizational information sharing information communication and inter-firm relationships

together represent process integration capabilities (De Vass, 2018). The inter and intra

14

organizational communication and information exchange are perceived to be facilitated by IoT capability. Organizational capability theory related to resource-based view theory suggests that a firm must develop its own resources and capabilities for performance improvement (Huo, 2012). Integration is a higher order process capability that can directly influence firm performance (Huo, 2012). Organizational capability theory also suggests that internal integration can directly affect external integration where internal process integration is the base for the development of the firm's external process integration (Huo, 2012). Verona (1999) suggest that internal capabilities include internal communication, process integration and job training, while external capabilities represent external communication and networks of partners. ICT implementation itself cannot have a direct effect on performance; rather it needs to be blended with the other organizational resources for performance improvement. Hence, IoT can improvs the integration capability of an organization as ICT (De Vass, 2018).

2.7.2 Systems Theory

In this study, systems theory is applied for analyzing the interconnectivity between the components of the supply chain integration and performance. This provides the basis for literature review and development of a conceptual framework. Systems theory and organizations Competitiveness in organizations depends on the ability to manage internal and external relationships. This requires establishing effective communication channels and information flow mechanisms to allow dynamic interactions with other business systems (Fatorachian, & Kazemi, 2021). Systems theory considers firms as holistic systems with a high level of integration and communication between the system components that are involved in the value creation process (Fatorachian, & Kazemi, 2021). So, based on systems theory, organizations are seen as

15

interconnected processes with a high level of integration and information sharing between business processes. Systems thinking and systemic understanding enables identifying system components and their relationships to each other and allow for analyzing the relationships between organizations and their surrounding environment (Rich and Piercy 2013). This results in understanding how the elements and components of a system interact and allows for understanding the dynamic behaviour of the supply chain system. Systems theory and supply chain performance According to Gorane and Kant (2015), successful supply chain integration requires analyzing and improving both individual and organizations performance and the entire supply chain integration. This calls for a holistic approach to supply chain integration (Fatorachian, & Kazemi, 2021).

CHAPTER THREE

RESEARCH METHODOLOGY

3.0 Introduction

The current chapter outlines the methods used to achieve the objectives of the study. It explains the methodology used. The main sections include research design, sampling design, method of data collection, data analysis and ethical considerations

3.1 Research Design

Descriptive, exploratory, and causal are types of research design. The selection of a type depends on the purpose and objectives of the study. This study adopted a descriptive survey research design, the reason being that it is appropriateness for social scientists, this study adopts the survey research approach as a means of collecting primary data from respondents as well as collecting primary data from large populations to be specifically observed. Surveys are known to be effective in gathering information on people's views, behaviour and definitions as well as relationships of cause and effect (Saunders et al, 2011). It is the use of questionnaires or interview strategies in documenting respondents' verbal behaviours. Surveys are frequently and widely used technique in giving feedback to 'who',' what',' where',' how much' and 'how many' in organizational and management research, according to Saunders et al (2011).

This study found it important to choose a method to execute the objectives of the research. There are different methods for such execution namely quantitative and qualitative methods. According to Zikmund (2000), the main purpose of quantitative method is to find out the link among two variables where one is the dependent and the other independent variable. The quantitative method is used for researches in natural science which explains the granger causal relationship of variables for regression and predictions. They normally involve in huge samples that demands more statistical techniques. It has statistical tools like t statistics, p values, F statistics and z statistics and others for making decisions on hypotheses which also shows how significant the variables play a role (Zikmund, 2000). On the other side of the coin, the qualitative method is subjective in nature and is characterised by the nearness to the object of research (Zikmund, 2000). According to Zikmund (2000), most researches do not focus on quantities but values that the researcher places on a particular variable. It aims at demonstrating a picture of events or situations in relation to the investigations. It also provides more information and prerequisites for deeper knowledge of current problem and its findings are most at times not statistically reviewed (Zikmund, 2000).

The focus of this study is to assess the relationship among internet of things, supply chain integration and performance in the automotive industry of Germany, therefore, quantitative method using descriptive and inferential statistics was adopted.

3.2 Research paradigm

"A paradigm is a body of propositions that describe how the world is conceptualized; it offers researchers and social scientists in general a Cosmo vision, which is a worldview and a means of demystifying the complexities of the real world and stating what is significant, necessary, legal, and reasonable (Guba, 1990). The idea put forth by Easterby et al. (2012) that there are two main research ideologies—positivist and phenomenological or social constructionist is advanced. The phenomenological ideology is qualitative and non-positivist, in contrast to the positivist ideology's empirical and quantitative nature. The core tenet of the positivist paradigm, according to Easterby

18

et al. (2012), is that the social world is an objective reality and that, as opposed to being inferred subjectively through sensation, reflection, or inference, its qualities can be objectively examined using empirical methods. It is also assumed that positivism is analogous to quantitative procedures since positivism comprises ontological and epistemological principles that elucidate how analysis can be carried out using these methods. The positivist philosophical framework, according to Saunders et al. (2009), also presupposes that the researcher is independent of the analysis and that it is neither influenced nor impacted by it. The positivist theory, which is empirical in character, analyzes statistics and applies statistical methods to research. The researcher assumes the position of an impartial observer, quietly developing detached interpretations of the information gathered in a manner that appears to be devoid of values. By examining the consistency and causal connections between variables in a sample, quantitative analysis seeks to explain and forecast what occurs in social settings.

The research questions being addressed and prior literature have led to the positivist method's selection. The positivist approach locates explanations for a problem based on a deductive process. The primary goal of this study is to examine the impact of internet of things on supply chain integration and performance. A positivist strategy is adopted for the study since it incorporates research on cultural and demographic aspects.

3.3 Population of the study

Nanevie (2012) define a population as the group of people, events, or things of interest that the researcher wants to investigate. Blumberg et al. (2014) explained population as all the components that meet the basis for inclusion in a study. The two types are a target and accessible population. The target population includes all members of a hypothetical set of people events or objects from

19

which research findings can be generalized while the accessible population is made up of all the individuals who realistically could be us in the research (Gall et al 2014). The population of the study comprises the employees of the Mercedes automotive industry in Germany. The scope of the research focused on the above mentioned industry because of their reputation in the automotive industry, their strategic location in the country call for major economic activities and ease of access to the employees.

3.4 Sampling Size and Technique

Sampling is an integral part of any empirical research and is associated with the selection of the correct individuals, events, or objects from which the required information is collected (Gray, 2019). It is a way to select a subset of a population to make statistical inferences from and to evaluate the characteristics of the whole population. Using the right sampling methods reduces research costs and provides greater flexibility, accuracy, and efficiency (Cochran, 1953). The two sampling types are probability sampling and nonprobability sampling. Both have advantages and disadvantages and the use of each depends on the goals of the researcher about data collection and validity.

A sample size of 50 employees from the Mercedes automotive industry in Germany was selected using probability sampling technique due to the aim of the study. The probability sampling technique was used since it was practically unfeasible to obtain the sample frame of all Mercedes automotive industry in Germany employees across Germany. The probability sampling technique reduces sampling bias, creates accurate sampling, and gives higher quality data collection, though it is time-consuming and expensive. Simple random sampling was used to select the actual sample size estimated.

3.5 Questionnaire Design and Data Collection Instrument

A survey instrument was developed to test the research model. The researcher used a self-administered questionnaire distributed to the employees of the Mercedes automotive industry in Germany. Although some respondents may be biased in answering the questions in the attempt to keep privacy, others may misunderstand the questions asked and give wrong feedback. A questionnaire was used due to the size of the sample population, which spreads over a large territory, it is economical and the best method of collecting information, it also put less pressure on the respondents for an immediate response (Manfreda, et al., 2002). The questionnaire comprises two parts. The first part includes the items related to demographic measurement. This part consists of the items that captured general information about the respondents such as gender, age, position, educational background and number of years spent with the company. This part of the questionnaire was designed using the interval scale. The demographics provided a better understanding of the responses from the respondents.

In the second part, questions are related to internet of thing, supply chain integration and employee performance variables. The study used three sets of questionnaires: (1) Internet of thing measuring instrument adapted from De Vass, et al (2018) which is a 12 item scale. (2) Supply chain integration instrument adapted from De Vass, et al (2018) a 10 item scale. (3) Performance scale adapted from De Vass, et al (2018) which is also a 10 item scale. This part of the questionnaire was designed by using a five-point Likert scale (1- "strongly agree" and 5 - "strongly disagree"). Five-point Likert scale was used since it considers the reliability of the respondents in a survey, expectation is that the 5 point scale might do better compared to other measuring scales owing to the choice of items on a scale identified by the construct of the survey. The 5 point scale gives more varieties of options which increase the probability of meeting the objective reality of people.

21

This scale also discloses more description about the research objective and appeals practically to the participants' faculty of reasoning (Pearse 2011).

3.6 Data Sources and Collection Procedure

This research study draws its data from only primary data sources. The primary data sources refer to data collected and analysed by the researcher from the field. The main primary data for the study was the responses obtained from respondents through questionnaires. The data obtained from these sources was scrutinized for suitability, reliability, adequacy and accuracy. The researcher used primary source data collection of standardized questionnaires. The standardized questionnaire was used to get answers, 'and unbiased opinion. Such instruments of data collection make it quite easy for participants to have the details required for the study.

An empirical study has been conducted in the Mercedes automotive industry of Germany. The population of the study was the employees from the Mercedes automotive industry. 65 questionnaires were administered to the employees of Mercedes automotive industry in Germany with the assistance of the marketing manager. The distribution and collection process lasted for one month and 55 questionnaires were received. 5 questionnaires were discarded from data collection usage due to difficulties in providing the right answers to the questionnaires. The procedure resulted in 50 usable questionnaires (response rate of 76.9%).

3.7 Data analysis

The analysis of the data was done using the STATA version 15.0 and Statistical Package for Social Science (SPSS) version 20.0 statistical software. The statistical software required the data collected to be numerically coded. Numerical codes were assigned to the majority of question prior to the administration of the questionnaire. The authors followed four key processes in analysing the data. Firstly, the questionnaires were screened and the appropriate ones were entered into the database. Secondly, the consistency and stability of the data were verified by calculating the coefficient of the fractal dimension using SPSS software. Thirdly, the author established the authenticity and relevance of the construct validity of the scales by conducting confirmatory factor analyses (CFA). Lastly, the hypotheses were tested for direct effects using multiple linear regression models.

3.8 Ethical considerations

Ethical issues are essential when studies involving human beings are conducted. According to Cavan (2001), ethics has been characterized as "a matter of principled sensitivity to the rights of others" and that "while truth is good, respect for human dignity is better". He admonished researchers to protect human rights, direct them, and oversee people's interests. According to Christians (2000), informed consent, privacy and confidentiality, and accuracy are the minimum considerations. All ethical requirements were followed in this study throughout all phases of the research. Before the data collection, the researcher sought permission from the Mercedes automotive industry of Germany. The participants were asked to participate willingly and offered the chance to withdraw from participation. Participants were informed that their feedback will be treated anonymous and with the needed confidentiality. Furthermore, participants were assured

23

that the data collected will not be used for any purpose other than that specified in the objectives of the study, which is intended solely for academic research. In particular, ethical concerns were addressed using the approach of informed consent and the confidentiality of participants.

CHAPTER FOUR

DATA ANALYSES AND DISCUSSION OF FINDINGS

4.0 Introduction

This section of the work presents the outcomes of the results. It presents descriptive statistics such as mean, standard deviation, minimum and maximum. It also presents the validity and reliability by conducting confirmatory factor analysis (CFA), exploratory factor analysis (EFA), average variance extracted (AVE), inter-factor correlations, and composite reliability (CR). Finally, model fitness and multi collinearity tests were presented. The data analysis and the discussion of the findings are therefore structured around the hypothesis.

.

4.1 Evaluation of Common Method Variance (CMV)

Common Method Variance (CMV) is one of the critical issues arising in current research. As a result, it is important to control for CMV in this study (Rodríguez-Ardura & Meseguer-Artola, 2020). Based on the literature, this study followed three main approaches in dealing with CMV. Firstly, the questionnaire was pretested to reduce ambiguity and verify its validity and reliability. Secondly, the participants were informed about the anonymity and confidentiality of their responses. Similarly, evaluation anxiety was minimized during data collection. Finally, Hermen's single factor test in an exploratory factor analysis (EFA) framework was conducted. Following Fuller et al. (2016)'s recommendation to examine the number of unrotated factor solutions, the number of components matrix was following the variables of the study with an eigenvalue greater than one (1). The total variance explained was 79.28%. The largest factor explained 20.39% of the variance suggesting that no single factor explained more than half of the total variance. This signifies that CMV was not a problem in this study.

4.2 Descriptive Statistics

Tables 4.1 present the descriptive statistics results of the study. The author used STATA version 15.0 to perform the descriptive statistics for the variables.

Table 4.1: Descriptive Statistics and Composite Reliability

Variable	CR	Obs	Mean	Std. Dev.	Min	Max
IoT	0.80	579	2.523	0.988	1	5
SCI	0.79	579	2.658	0.993	1	5
PER	0.85	579	2.993	1.565	1	5

According to Table 4.1 above, the study used valid responses from 50 participants. As indicated earlier, the study used a five-point Likert scale ranging from 1-5 ratings for collecting the data. According to Table 4.1, all the variables understudy namely IoT, SCI and PER recorded a minimum of one (1) and a maximum of five (5). In terms of mean and standard deviation, the participants relatively scored the variables of interest, suggesting that PER in the German automotive industry is relatively high with the mean score (M=2.993, SD=1.565) while IoT had the lowest mean score (M=2.523, SD=0.988). SCI had mean scores (M=2.658, SD=0.993).

4.3 Reliability and Validity of the Constructs

The consistency, stability, and reproducibility of measurement results are concerned with reliability. Conforming to Field (2009), a scale should consistently represent the construct it is

26

measuring in the reliability calculation. Besides using the coefficient alpha (Cronbach's alpha) the internal accuracy and consistency of the scales is also calculated. Theoretically, Cronbach alpha looks at inter-relationships between the objects intended to measure a construct. According to Field (2009), an appropriate value is the Cronbach alpha with a value between 0.7 and 0.8; values significantly lower imply an inaccurate scale. In the same way, Hair, et al. (2010) postulates that for most research purposes, a coefficient alpha greater than 0.7 is highly satisfactory. Nonetheless, in the early phase of the analysis, Nunnally (1978) argue that a coefficient alpha of 0.5 to 0.6 was satisfactory. The researcher adopted a positivist model of analysis for this research study, which is an appropriate way to collect data for defined variables of interest. The investigator designed the survey instrument to gather data from the staff of the Ghana telecommunication industry. In this analysis, with the aid of Cronbach's alpha, the investigator assessed internal reliability, and validity. Validity decides the extent to which a construct and its corresponding measurement indicators are linked and the extent to which the construct they were intended to measure is reflected in this set of items (Hair, et al., and 2010). As a general practice in many social science studies, this study conducted both confirmatory factor analysis and exploratory factor analysis to test the validity and reliability of the instruments used.

4.3.1 Standardized Factor Loadings and T Values

The influential nature of Confirmatory factor analysis (CFA) as a statistical tool for probing the nature of and relationships among latent constructs is highly regarded among researchers. Since it helps to measure the construct validity, identify method effects, and helps in evaluating the factor invariance through time and groups (Brown, 2014),. The use of CFA continues to gain ground in the psychological literature because of the belief researchers have in the Structural Equation Model as a robust model specifically. Given the critical impact CFA makes in the measure development

27

and due to the understanding that having a tool that manages the measurement of variables effectively, it can be presumed to be paramount quantitatively only because its role is crucial to the results a researcher reports. The CFA performed on the variables understudy in this research proved that all the standardized factor loadings were above 0.60 and the t-values are significant for all the items in table 4.2.

Table 4.2: CFA Standardized Factor Loadings and T Values

Construct	Items	β	t value	Composite Reliabilities (CR)	Cronbach Alpha (α)
Internet of Thing	IoT1	0.656	22.230	0.803	0.793
	IoT2	0.737	28.520		
	IoT3	0.753	30.070		
	IoT4	0.647	21.650		
	IoT5	0.637	15.510		
	IoT6	0.675	23.300		
	IoT7	0.750	29.210		
	IoT8	0.604	18.740		
	IoT9	0.634	15.170		
	IoT10	0.819	39.610		
	IoT11	0.810	38.520		
	IoT12	0.733	31.340		
Supply Chain Integration	SCI1	0.716	29.060	0.854	0.818
	SCI 2	0.728	30.260		
	SCI 3	0.779	36.610		
	SCI 4	0.674	25.060		
	SCI 5	0.691	26.370		
	SCI 6	0.641	16.260		
	SCI 7	0.736	29.660		
	SCI 8	0.776	34.080		

	SCI 9	0.736	29.750		
	SCI 10	0.654	22.710		
Performance	P1	0.639	21.970	0.864	0.853
	P2	0.735	30.170		
	P3	0.697	26.590		
	P4	0.717	28.410		
	P5	0.694	26.230		
	P6	0.699	19.270		
	P7	0.746	32.660		
	P8	0.780	37.190		
	P9	0.767	35.370		

4.3.2 Correlation Matrix and Average Variance Extracted (AVE)

In addition to the CFA, this study performed correlations among the variables and the square of AVE. The results are presented in Table 4.3.

Table 4.3: Correlation Matrix and Average Variance Extracted

Variable	AVE	IoT	SCI	PER
IoT	.579	**.761**		
SCI	.581	0.29	**.762**	
PER	.542	0.12	0.27	**.736**

The correlation results in Table 4.3 show that internet of thing correlated positively with supply chain integration and performance. In the same vain, supply chain integration correlated positively with performance In addition, the average variance extracted (AVE) for the scales ranged from 0.542 – 0.581 in table 4.3. This shows that the values were greater than the recommended threshold of 0.50 for acceptable AVE indicating evidence of convergence validity (Gaskin & Lim, (2016). It was also proved in this table that the square root of the AVE values ranged from 0.761 – 0.736

29

which were high above the inter-factor correlations among the constructs providing strong evidence of discriminant validity. These were all above the reliability threshold (0.7) generally recommended for using an instrument (Fornell, & Larcker, 1981) suggesting that the instruments are reliable. Also, all the correlation values were below 0.70 suggesting absence of potential collinearity among the explanatory variables.

4.3.3 Model Fitness

Similarly, the results of the model fits from the CFA analysis by AMOS (V 22.0) disclosed that the overall goodness of fits indices including goodness-of-fit index (GFI) 0.926, adjusted goodness-of-fit index (AGFI) 0.961, comparative fit index (CFI) 0.943, root mean square error of approximation (RMSEA) 0.047 and χ^2/df were within the acceptable level for model fit. From the model fitness, it is therefore deduced that the model for that study is a good fit for the data.

4.3.4 Kaiser-Meyer-Olkin (KMO) Barlet's Test (BT)

To measure the sampling adequacy for individual variables and complete the model, the KMO and BT were performed. The results in Table 4.4 convey that the KMO value is 0.851which is above the minimum recommended threshold for proceeding to factor analysis. The BT value is relatively large with sig. value of 0.000 rejecting the null hypothesis that the variables are not inter-correlated.

Table 4.4 Kaiser-Meyer-Olkin and Bartlett's Test

KMO Measure of Sampling Adequacy		0.851
	Chi-square	4819.859
BT of Sphericity	Df	54
	Sig.	0.000

30

4.3.5 Rotated Component Matrix

The rotated component matrix aids in ascertaining what the components loadings signify. Table 4.5 presents the results of the rotated matrix. The results show that, the rotated component loaded under 3 different items.

Table 4.5 Rotated Component Matrix

items	Rotated Matrix		
	1	2	3
IoT1	0.818		
IoT2	0.811		
IoT3	0.827		
IoT4	0.867		
IoT5	0.713		
IoT6	0.709		
IoT7	0.657		
IoT8	0.745		
IoT9	0.836		
IoT10	0.796		
IoT11	0.665		
IoT12	0.758		
SCI1		0.702	

SCI 2		0.673	
SCI 3		0.681	
SCI 4		0.731	
SCI 5		0.802	
SCI 6		0.711	
SCI 7		0.795	
SCI 8		0.678	
SCI 9		0.801	
SCI 10		0.841	
P1			0.858
P2			0.771
P3			0.834
P4			0.745
P5			0.811
P6			0.724
P7			0.834
P8			0.723
P9			0.713

4.4 Multi-collinearity Test

Multi-collinearity is the evaluation of a variable that can be explained by other variables in the analysis (Hair, et al., 2010). It is a correlation matrix problem in which three or more independent variables are strongly correlated with each other (0.9 or higher) (Hair, et al., 2010; Tabachnick and Fidell, 2007). The existence of a higher multi-collinearity degree decreases the unique variance described by each independent variable (β-value) and increases the percentage of the mutual prediction (Hair, et al., 2010). This implies that the existence of multi-collinearity limits the regression value size and become difficult to comprehend each individual independent variable's contribution (Field, 2009). Two common methods are used to detect multi-collinearity, firstly by examining the matrix of multivariate and bivariate correlation and, secondly, by calculating the impact of variance inflation factors (VIF) and tolerance (Pallant, 2010; Field, 2009; Tabachnick and Fidell, 2007). According to Pallant (2010), tolerance is an indicator of how much of the variability of the specified independent is not explained by the other independent variables in the model, while VIF is the inverse of the tolerance effect. The greater the VIF and the lower the tolerance (0.1) show that multi-collinearity is present (Pallant, 2010). The next step of the regression analysis was to verify that multi-collinearity was not a problem in this study. Table 4.6 below presents the results of the multi-collinearity test.

Table 4.6 Multi-collinearity Results

Variable	Performance		Supply Chain Integration	
	Tolerance	VIF	Tolerance	VIF
Gender	.848	1.179	.415	2.408

Age	.676	1.478	.257	3.895
Educational background	.836	1.196	.497	2.013
Position	.737	1.358	.827	1.210
Experience	.856	1.168	.856	1.168
IoT	.747	1.339	.747	1.339

The dependent variables were performance and supply chain integration.

Multi-collinearity is present where tolerance value is less than 0.2 and the VIF value is greater than five (5), otherwise there is no multi-collinearity. According to Table 4.6, the collinearity statistics for Tolerance for both performance and supply chain integration are all greater than 0.2 which is the threshold. Furthermore, the Variance Inflation Factor (VIF) for both performance and supply chain integration equations are all less than five (5) suggesting that multi-collinearity does not exist in this study.

4.5 Analysis of the Effect of Internet of Thing on Supply chain performance.

Using Internet of Thing as the independent variable and conditioning all other supply chain integration determinants such as age, gender, region, company, educational background, position, experience and IoT, the results in Model 2 of Table 4.7 below revealed that Internet of Thing positively influences supply chain integration in the Mercedes automotive industry in Germany. This is to say that a percentage increase in Internet of Thing in the automotive industry will lead to an increase in supply chain integration. This outcome is in favor of H1. Thus, these results provide further evidence to support hypotheses H1 which states that Internet of Thing has positive impact on supply chain integration.

34

Table 4.7: The effect of Internet of Thing on Supply chain performance

Variables	Supply chain performance					
	Model 1			Model 2		
	Estimates	S.E	C.R	Estimates	S.E	C.R
Constant	0.741***	0.218	3.402	0.651***	0.227	2.861
Gender	0.116***	0.042	2.760	0.102**	0.044	2.321
Age	0.192***	0.035	5.565	0.169***	0.036	4.680
Educational background	0.180***	0.044	4.093	0.158***	0.046	3.442
Position	0.195***	0.043	4.536	0.171***	0.042	4.040
Experience	0.217***	0.045	4.825	0.191***	0.043	4.404
IoT	0.151***	0.041	3.639	0.133***	0.043	3.060
F-test	89.56***			84.44***		
R-squared	0.571			0.596		
Adj R-squar	0.563			0.588		
Obs	579			579		

***,** indicates significant at 1% and 5% levels of significance respectively

4.6 Analysis of the Effect of Internet of Thing on Performance

According to Table 4.8 above, the results in model 1 present the control variables including gender, age, educational background, experience and position. In the same vain, the results in model 1 reveal that conditioning other Performance determinants such as gender, age, educational background, experience, and position influence Performance. In Model 2, the results show that Internet of Thing (**IoT**) has a positive influence on Performance. Thus, improvement in Internet of Thing will increase performance. This finding supports H2, which states that 1 Internet of Thing has positive effect on performance.

Table 4.8: The effect of Internet of Thing on Performance

Variables	Performance					
	Model 1			Model 2		
	Estimates	S.E	C.R	Estimates	S.E	C.R
Constant	0.532**	0.227	2.344	0.805***	0.252	3.193
Gender	0.123**	0.060	2.043	0.126**	0.060	2.088
Age	0.209***	0.040	5.256	0.209***	0.040	5.279
Educational backgd	0.193**	0.051	3.782	0.196***	0.051	3.829
Position	0.429***	0.028	15.435	0.420***	0.028	15.096
Experience	0.215***	0.047	4.582	0.212**	0.047	4.537
IoT				0.125***	0.035	3.596
F-test	104.63***			62.76***		
R-squared	0.562			0.571		
Adj R-squar	0.557			0.562		

Obs	50			50		

***,** indicates significant at 1% and 5% levels of significance respectively

4.7 Analysis of the Effect of Supply Chain Integration on Performance

According to table 4.9 below, model 1 presents the results of the control variables for performance. The findings in model 2 of Table 4.9 revealed that supply chain integration positively influences performance, indicating that an improvement in supply chain integration will induce an increase in performance. This is in favour of H3.

Table 4.9: The effect of Supply Chain Integration on Performance

Variables	Performance					
	Model 1			Model 2		
	Estimates	S.E	C.R	Estimates	S.E	C.R
Constant	1.737***	0.361	4.815	0.918**	0.374	2.452
Gender	0.045***	0.010	4.409	0.097**	0.043	2.257
Age	0.060**	0.029	2.069	0.082**	0.039	2.117
Educational background	0.14***	0.041	3.392	0.084**	0.036	2.344
Position	0.133**	0.055	2.448	0.077**	0.055	2.213
Experience	0.083**	0.036	2.299	0.081**	0.040	2.025

SCI				0.151***	0.052	2.907
F-test	1.52**			9.05***		
R-squared	0.018			0.161		
Adj R-squar	0.006			0.143		
Obs	50			50		

***,**indicates significant at 1% and 5% levels of significance respectively

4.8 Discussions of Findings

The study seeks to examine the effect of Internet of Thing on supply chain integration and performance. The outcome of this study indicates that Internet of Thing had a significant and positive effect on supply chain integration performance in the Mercedes automotive industry, Germany. This result is consistent with the findings of Rejeb, et al., (2020), Tu, (2018), Vanpoucke, et al., (2017) which found a positive relationship between Internet of Thing and supply chain integration. Again, the findings of this study indicate that Internet of Thing had a significant positive effect on performance in the Mercedes automotive industry, Germany. This result is similar to that of De Vass, et al., (2018), Kahlert, et al., (2017), Borgia, (2014) which found out that Internet of Thing has positive and significant impact of performance. Furthermore, this study has found out that supply chain integration in the Mercedes automotive industry, Germany has significant and positive effect on performance. This finding is in line with the findings of (Owuso, & Jaja, 2022; Cruz, A. 2021, De Vass, et al., 2018, Shee et al. 2018; Vanpoucke et al. 2017) which stated that Internet of Thing has a positive relationship with performance.

The positive effect of IoT on supply chain integration and performance in the automotive industry was achieved due to policies and procedures adopted by the Mercedes Company in dealing with their suppliers, customers and employees. The company provides adequate support for their suppliers and employees to work to meet their needs and requirements. It can be argued that IoT-enabled external integration is related at a higher significance for supply chain performance gains beyond firm boundaries due to IoT's pervasiveness and omnipresent ability. Further, the automotive industry has linked existing IoT devices with suppliers and customers, mustering all digital data into one Internet-based platform to share, communicate and process information from each other. This unified supply chain system approach has also derived greater benefits for all partners fulfilling the conceptual objective of IoT platform to establishing a dynamic network. Again, previous studies have concluded that IoT contributes to policy making by providing evidence that the investment in IoT is a sound public investment. Therefore, various developed and developing countries have pursued national strategies on IoT technology deployment and allocated substantial funding on IoT research which advocates IoT to be lifted to the national strategy for the automotive industry.

4.9 summary of research hypothesis

Attempts were made to determine the effect of Internet of Thing on supply chain integration and performance and the effect of supply chain integration on performance in the German automotive industry specifically Mercedes. A multiple regression analysis was calculated using supply chain integration and performance as a dependent variables and Internet of Thing and supply chain integration as the independent variables. Table 4.7 - 4.9 give the picture of what was obtained. The results showed that Internet of Thing has significant impacts on supply chain integration and performance (p<0.05) and supply chain integration had significant impact on performance (p<0.005). This means that Internet of Thing and supply chain integration jointly determine performance in the automotive industry. It is concluded that H1and H2 are supported. In the same vain supply chain integration influences performance, which concluded that, H3 is supported.

Table 4.10: The summary result of hypothesis testing

No.	Hypothesis	Decision
H1	Internet of Thing has positive effect on supply chain integration.	Supported
H2	Internet of Thing has positive effect on performance.	Supported
H3	supply chain integration has positive effect on performance	Supported

CHAPTER FIVE

CONCLUSIONS AND RECOMMENDATIONS

The previous chapter presents the results of data analyses and discussion of the findings. This chapter consists of four parts, which are conclusions of the findings, academic and managerial implications, limitation and recommendation for future research and conclusion.

5.1 Conclusions of the study

Many companies to manage the supply chain integration and improve performance within the organization have used Internet of Things. To improve supply chain integration and performance effectiveness, efficiency and flexibility, most organisations realized the importance of taking the ICT needs into account. IoT has emerged as an innovative technology with capabilities to improve supply chain information flow. However, the effect of IoT on supply chain integration and in turn performance is not yet fully explored empirically.

The main purpose of this study was to assess the effect of Internet of Thing on supply chain integration and performance and the impact of supply chain integration on performance in the Mercedes automotive industry, Germany through questionnaire. 50 questionnaires were received and analysed. Based on the review of the literature, a model was developed for the study. In all, the three main hypotheses were tested. The data was subjected to statistical analysis by using STATA statistical software. The performed descriptive statistics, correlation and linear regression analysis. The study attempted to find the effect of Internet of Thing on supply chain integration and performance. The findings of the study concluded that Internet of Thing had a significant and positive effect on supply chain integration in the Mercedes automotive industry, Germany. Again, the findings of this study indicate that Internet of Thing had a significant positive effect on

41

performance in the Mercedes automotive industry, Germany. Consequentially, this study has found out that supply chain integration in the Mercedes automotive industry, Germany has significant and positive effect on performance.

5.2 Theoretical and managerial implications

The outcome of this research provides empirical evidence for the effect of Internet of Thing on supply chain integration and performance in the Mercedes automotive industry of Germany. Also, although Internet of Thing and supply chain integration studies encourage methodological diversity, quantitative methods research is rarely utilized. Moreover, studies linking both Internet of Thing and supply chain integration are rare. Therefore, this research advances Internet of Thing and supply chain integration research by using quantitative research methods to offer empirical evidence to validate and explain how Internet of Thing and supply chain integration improve the performance of the entire automotive industry. Further, the literature is so far limited to Internet of Thing technology applications. This study has examined Internet of Thing in an empirical framework to analyze its significant effects on performance improvement. Therefore, Internet of Thing and supply chain integration for improving supply chain integration and performance is unique in this research. In addition, this study proposed a modified conceptual framework on the relationship between Internet of Thing, supply chain integration and performance based on related literature which no study has explored. This offers theoretical support for the adoption and implementation of this framework for future studies.

5.3 Recommendation of the study

The study makes the following recommendations, which aim at helping governments, stakeholders and managers in the automotive industry especially the Mercedes automotive industry of Germany to provide effective strategies that build strong Internet of Thing and supply chain integration to improve performance. It is therefore, recommended that stakeholders and managers of the automotive industry should create a conducive business environment and the necessary support for Internet of Thing and supply chain integration. This will be helpful in the improvement of performance in the automotive industry fraternity. Again, technologies are given a high priority in government agendas. Internet of Thing has an infinite potential and the economic value from Internet of Thing is anticipated to generate a rapid GDP increase, therefore, enthusiasm of many governments is deeply immersed by this emerging paradigm. As a prevailing technology is gathering its momentum of everything on digital world, therefore this study recommends that all governments around the world to patronize the Internet of Thing revolution strategy. It is also recommended that the stakeholders in the automotive business who are looking for better performances should pay much attention in strengthening their internet of thing and supply chain integration since the result of this study indicated that, there is a positive relationship between internet of thing, supply chain integration and performance in the automotive industry.

5.4 Limitations and recommendation for future research

This study has deepened the theoretical and empirical research on capacity building, new media and business performance in the Multimedia Group Limited. However, there are unquestionably some limitations and future research directions, which require consideration to suitably position the outcomes of the study. Firstly, the sampling frame for this study was limited to only 50 employees and was done in a particular country (Germany) and specifically in the Mercedes automotive industry, which limits the generalizability of the findings. Upcoming studies using data from different countries may additionally assist expand the generalizability of these outcomes. Secondly, cross-sectional data was used. Cross-sectional research suffers from incapacity to ascertain the causes and effects of the investigated variables. Even though the hypothesized causal ordering is possible, the cross-sectional layout limits our capability to draw a causal conclusion. Future studies therefore should use longitudinal data to increase confidence within the causal nature of the relationships examined in this study. Furthermore, the study adopted questionnaire as a tool for data collection. The other data collection methods had not been considered. As a result they may not be 100% accurate. It is recommended that future research utilize different sampling methods and data collection methods to ensure the generalizability of the findings.

REFERENCES

Agwu, E. (2018). Analysis of the impact of strategic management on the business performance of SMEs in Nigeria. *Academy of Strategic Management,* 17(1), 1-20.

Almatrooshi, B., Kumar S.S., Farouk, S. (2016) Determinants of organizational performance: a proposed framework. *International Journal of Productivity and Performance Management,* 65(6), 844 – 859

Battor, M., Battor, M. (2010): The impact of customer relationship management capability on innovation and performance advantages: testing a mediated model, *Journal of Marketing Management,* 26(9-10), 842-857

Ben-Daya, M., Hassini, E., & Bahroun, Z. (2017) Internet of things and supply chain management: a literature review. *International Journal of Production Research,* 1-24.

Borgia, E. (2014). The Internet of Things vision: Key features, applications and open issues. Computer Communications, 54, 1-31.

Brown, T. A. (2014). *Confirmatory factor analysis for applied research*: Guilford Publications.

Cavana, R. & Sekaran, D.B.L (2001). *Applied business research: Qualitative and quantitative methods.* Wiley Milton, Australia.

Christians, C. (2000). Ethics and politics in qualitative research', in Denzin, N.K and Lincoln, Y.S Disease 2019 (COVID-19) From Publicly Reported Confirmed Cases: Estimation and Application. https://doi.org/10.7326/M20-0504.

Cruz, A. (2021). Convergence between Blockchain and the Internet of Things. *International Journal of Technology, Innovation and Management (IJTIM),* 1(1), 34-53.

De Vass, T. (2018). *The "Internet of Things" enabled supply chain integration and performance: a mixed method investigation of the Australian retail industry* (Doctoral dissertation, Victoria University).

De Vass, T., Shee, H., & Miah, S. J. (2018). The effect of "Internet of Things" on supply chain integration and performance: An organisational capability perspective. *Australasian Journal of Information Systems, 22.*

Fatorachian, H., & Kazemi, H. (2021). Impact of Industry 4.0 on supply chain performance. *Production Planning & Control, 32*(1), 63-81.

Field, A. (2009). Discovering statistics using SPSS. 3rd edition. Sage Publications Limited.

Fuller, C. M., Simmering, M. J., Atinc, G., Atinc, Y. and Babin, B. J. (2016). Common methods variance detection in business research. Journal of Business Research, 69(8), 3192-3198.

Gorane, S. J., and R. Kant. 2015. "Supply Chain Practices." *International Journal of Productivity and Performance Management 64* (5): 657-685.

Guba, E. G. (1990). The paradigm dialog. In *Alternative paradigms conference, mar, 1989, indiana u, school of education, san francisco, ca, us.* Sage Publications, Inc.

Gupta, V. K., & Wales, W. J. (2017). Assessing organizational performance within entrepreneurial orientation research: Where have we been and where can we go from here? *The Journal of Entrepreneurship, 26*(1), 51-76.

Hair, J.F., Black, W.C., Babin, J.B., & Anderson, R.E. (2010). *Multivariate data analysis: A global perspective.* 7th edition. Upper Saddle River, New Jersey: Pearson Education.

Huo, B 2012, 'The impact of supply chain integration on company performance: an organizational capability perspective', *Supply Chain Management: An International Journal*, vol. 17, no. 6, pp. 596-610

Journal of Production Economics, 159(1), 29-40.

Kahlert, M., Constantinides, E., & de Vries, S. (2017). The relevance of technological autonomy in the customer acceptance of IoT services in retail. Paper presented at the Proceedings of the Second International Conference on Internet of things and Cloud Computing, Cambridge, United Kingdom.

Kim, HJ (2017) 'Information technology and firm performance: the role of supply chain integration', *Operations Management Research,* vol. 10, no. 1, pp. 1-9

Lee, I & Lee, K 2015, 'The Internet of Things (IoT): Applications, investments, and challenges for enterprises', *Business Horizons*, vol. 58, no. 4, pp. 431-40.

Li, B., & Li, Y. (2017). Internet of things drives supply chain innovation: A research framework. *International Journal of Organizational Innovation, 9*(3), 71-92.

Miorandi, D., Sicari, S., De Pellegrini, F., & Chlamtac, I. (2012). Internet of things: Vision, applications and research challenges. *Ad hoc networks, 10*(7), 1497-1516.

Mishra, D., Gunasekaran, A., Childe, S. J., Papadopoulos, T., Dubey, R., & Wamba, S. F. (2016). Vision, applications and future challenges of Internet of Things. Industrial Management & Data Systems, 116(7), 1331-1355.

Mishra, D., Gunasekaran, A., Childe, S. J., Papadopoulos, T., Dubey, R., & Wamba, S. F. (2016). Vision applications and future challenges of Internet of Things. *Industrial Management & Data Systems, 116*(7), 1331-1355.

Mohanty, S., & Mishra, P. C. (2020). Framework for understanding Internet of Things in human resource management. *Revista ESPACIOS, 41*(12).

Naser, H. A. N.(2019) The effect of "Internet of Things" on supply chain integration and performance: An organizational capability perspective.

47

Newman, D.L. & Brown, R.D. (1995). *Applied ethics for program evaluation.* Sage Publications, Incorporated.

Nunnally, J. (1978). Psychometric methods. New York, NY: McGraw-Hill.

of Things for order fulfillment in a collaborative warehousing environment. International

Owuso, S. M., & Jaja, H. (2022). Effect of Technology on Supply Chain Performance of Courier Firm in Nigeria: Implication for Post Pandemic Era. *Int. J. Res. Educ. Sustain. Dev, 2,* 32-42.

Pallant, J. (2010) *SPSS survival manual.* 4th edition. Berkshire, UK: McGraw-Hill.

Prajogo, D., & Olhager, J. (2012). Supply chain integration and performance: The effects of long-term relationships, information technology and sharing, and logistics integration. *International Journal of Production Economics, 135*(1), 514-522.

Reaidy, P. J., Gunasekaran, A., & Spalanzani, A. (2015). Bottom-up approach based on Internet

Rejeb, A., Simske, S., Rejeb, K., Treiblmaier, H., & Zailani, S. (2020). Internet of Things research in supply chain management and logistics: A bibliometric analysis. *Internet of Things, 12,* 100318.

Rich, N. and N. Piercy. 2013. "Losing patients: a systems view on healthcare improvement." *Production Planning & Control 24* (10-11): 962-975.

Tabachnick, B.G., & Fidell, L.S. (2007). *Using multivariate statistics.* 5th edition. London: Pearson International.

Tang, C. S., & Veelenturf, L. P. (2019). The strategic role of logistics in the industry 4.0 era. *Transportation Research Part E: Logistics and Transportation Review, 129,* 1-11.

Tu, M. (2018). An exploratory study of Internet of Things (IoT) adoption intention in logistics and supply chain management-a mixed research approach. International Journal of Logistics Management, The(just-accepted), 00-00.

Uckelmann, D., Harrison, M., & Michahelles, F. (2011). An architectural approach towards the future internet of things. In *Architecting the internet of things* (pp. 1-24). Springer, Berlin, Heidelberg.

Vanpoucke, E., Vereecke, A., & Muylle, S. (2017). Leveraging the impact of supply chain integration through information technology. International Journal of Operations & Production Management, 37(4), 510-530.

Verdouw, CN, Beulens, AJM, Reijers, HA & van der Vorst, JGAJ (2016) 'A control model for object virtualization in supply chain management', Computers in Industry, vol. 68, pp. 116-31.

Yu, W, Jacobs, MA, Chavez, R & Feng, M (2017) The impacts of IT capability and marketing capability on supply chain integration: a resource-based perspective', *International Journal of Production Research*, vol. 55, no. 14, pp. 4196-211.

Zhang, X, Pieter van Donk, D & van der Vaart, T (2011) 'Does ICT influence supply chain management and performance? A review of survey-based research', *International Journal of Operations & Production Management,* vol. 31, no. 11, pp. 1215-47.

Zikmund, W.G. (2000). Business research methods (6th Ed). Fort Worth TX: Dryden Press cop. cop.

APPENDIX QUESTIONNAIRE

The effect of "internet of things" on supply chain integration and performance

Please answer the following questions by marking the appropriate answer(s) circling (O). This questionnaire is strictly for research purpose only, therefore, all information provided shall be treated with maximum caution and confidentiality.

Thank you for your cooperation and the time spent in answering this questionnaire.

SECTION A: Personal Data

1. **Gender**   [ ] Male

   [ ] Female

2. **Age**   [ ] Below 20 yrs

   [ ] 20-39

   [ ] 40-59

   [ ] 60 and above

3. **Position**

[ ] Top management level employees

[ ] Middle management level employees

[ ] Lower management level employees

4. **Educational Background**

[ ] Secondary and Diploma

[ ] Degree

[ ] Post Graduate

Others……………………………..

5. **Experience of employees, state in years……………**

SECTION B

Instruction: Please circle (O) the number that represents your most appropriate answer.

Strongly Disagree	Disagree	Neutral	Agree	Strongly Agree
1	2	3	4	5

	Internet of Things					
1	IoT provides individual item level identification.	1	2	3	4	5
2	IoT provides unit level identification	1	2	3	4	5
3	IoT monitor, track and trace supply chain entities and people through autocaptured data.	1	2	3	4	5
4	IoT measures supply chain activities, processes and its environmental conditions	1	2	3	4	5
5	IoT helps control supply chain processes remotely.	1	2	3	4	5
6	IoT makes autonomous supply chain decisions.	1	2	3	4	5
7	IoT provides real-time information to optimize supply chain activities.	1	2	3	4	5

8	IoT provides real-time intelligence of supply chain operations.	1	2	3	4	5
9	IoT provides large volumes and variety of data to apply data analytics for tactical and strategic decision making.	1	2	3	4	5
10	IoT strengthens inter and intra organizational information sharing within the supply chain.	1	2	3	4	5
11	IoT facilitates inter and intra organizational decision making within the supply chain.	1	2	3	4	5
12	IoT strengthens communication and coordination between operators.	1	2	3	4	5
	Supply Chain Integration					
13	We have been able to improve information exchange in our supply chain.	1	2	3	4	5
14	We have been able to establish a quick ordering of inventory in our supply chain.	1	2	3	4	5
15	We accurately plan and adopt the procurement process and collaboration in our supply chain.	1	2	3	4	5
16	We have been able to stabilize procurement in our supply chain.	1	2	3	4	5
17	We share real-time demand forecasts in our supply chain.	1	2	3	4	5
18	We have been able to improve in strategic partnerships in our supply chain.	1	2	3	4	5
19	We help suppliers improve their processes to better meet our needs in our supply chain.	1	2	3	4	5
20	We have been able to improve the account payable processes for our suppliers.					

		1	2	3	4	5
21	We have been able to improve the transport/logistics processes of logistics partners to deliver orders just in time.	1	2	3	4	5
22	We have been able to improve in our receiving processes for delivered goods.	1	2	3	4	5
Performance						
23	We have been able to develop our organizational operations to improve the product delivery cycle time.	1	2	3	4	5
24	We have been able to develop our organizational operations to improve productivity.	1	2	3	4	5
25	We have been able to develop our organizational operations to improve sales of existing products.	1	2	3	4	5
26	We have been able to develop our organizational operations to find new revenue streams.	1	2	3	4	5
27	We have been able to develop our organizational operations to build strong and continuous bonds with customers.	1	2	3	4	5
28	We have been able to develop our organizational operations to gain precise knowledge of customer buying patterns.	1	2	3	4	5
29	We have been able to develop our organizational operations to improve customer satisfaction.	1	2	3	4	5
30	We have been able to develop our organizational operations to improve employee satisfaction	1	2	3	4	5
31	We have been able to develop our organizational operations to improve employee health and safety	1	2	3	4	5

YOUR KNOWLEDGE HAS VALUE

- We will publish your bachelor's and
  master's thesis, essays and papers

- Your own eBook and book -
  sold worldwide in all relevant shops

- Earn money with each sale

Upload your text at www.GRIN.com
and publish for free